In the Gemini Café
NEIL CAMPBELL

Newton-le-Willows

Published in the United Kingdom in 2019
by The Knives Forks And Spoons Press,
51 Pipit Avenue,
Newton-le-Willows,
Merseyside,
WA12 9RG.

ISBN 978-1-912211-24-1

Acknowledgements:

Some of these poems first appeared (in slightly different form) in *A
Quiet Courage, Eunoia Review, Ink, Sweat and Tears, Lamport
Court, Live from Worktown, Structo, The Open Mouse, The Stockholm
Review, The Lake, Beatification* and *Under the Radar*. My thanks to
the editors.

Thanks to three amigos for poetic inspiration: John G Hall, Steve
Waling, J Barret Wolf.

Supported using public funding by
**ARTS COUNCIL
ENGLAND**

LOTTERY FUNDED

for Nom

Monday comes, as it must, with a pale
moon sinking below the elms

— Philip Levine

Contents

Poem after One Bottle of Orchard Cider, 95p from Aldi

I couldn't take it
and that's why I drank it.
Within minutes the sky
was a miracle of light
and distant dreams appeared
among it, drifting brighter
towards the vainglorious moonlight
of words untrammelled, unfolded,
brought forth from the bright
caressing clouds and sky and air,
all opened and all blowing and feeling
and emerging from the clanking of
beer bottles, and emptying of cans,
and the poems of booze poured
forth and the solitude that prompted
them was reinforced in their writing,
so that the band aids of booze
joined together, became a kind of noose
of their own imagining, the dark
dilapidated surrounds returning
every morning with the traffic
taking people back to the
boring fucking jobs I'd never
believe in, those tombs of commerce,
catacombs of delusion, filled
with shopping bags to last
a lifetime.

Sacked Again

Once again the irony was lost and the curtain came down on another glittering career. I walked from the frightened eyes and the dull, disbelieving minds out onto the long road back towards the latest in a long line of bus stops. This time the workers were all going the other way towards jobs that were their prisons, while I, conceited, penniless, rising, lifted in my heart and escaping the shackles, looked anew at a glorious day, all mine again as I sat on the bus with the sun streaming through the windows and the wrinkled ticket smoothing in my hands.

Artist Saving for His Flight to Lahore

So we were three days into the training and this guy from PK googled a sea that's two different colours. I knew why he was showing me it. The picture was beautiful, pure poetry, different shades of green and blue with the Gibraltar sill between. It was salt water and sweet water.

And this guy, who was still living at home with his parents, and who was going to Lahore after the call centre job was over, and who was going to be an accountant after, and who sketched pictures on his pad throughout the training, said to me, 'that water, those colours, it's like a metaphor, innit.'

Bookmark

Ten years ago
I went to San Francisco.
City Lights first of course
but my bookmark is from Black Oak Books.
I look at the aged bookmark
with its green tree and red letters
and my own scribbles on the back:
random lyrical lines, ideas for stories.
It occurs to me that I haven't changed
though I tried to change.
I tried to change and I failed.
I tried to be good and I'm not.
I was drinking back then
in my own drinking way
sporadically and fulsomely and drunkenly
and today I realize
I've been listening to Kerouac
and re-reading my creased Bukowskis.
His poem 'Blue Collar Solitude'
rings the same bell for me now
as it did back then.
Looking back, I realize
that there is no more to this writing
than a solitary notebook, cheap pens
and the avoidance of work.

'Fantastic Opportunity'

So tomorrow I take the 'fantastic opportunity'
to work on the 5pm - 10.15pm shift
at the Manchester Mail Centre.
God knows I've done shit jobs before
but never with a contract like this.
Zero hours. £6.50 per hour.

Twenty years ago I worked in a warehouse
on a better rate
and I got paid if I was off sick.
It will be cracking the flags tomorrow,
the whole city will be in sunshine
and I will be inside, sorting mail,
still hoping for the glimpse of a woman.

The Only Sun in the Place

The manager,
a little Turkish fella
called Sol
had already been called
both a poison dwarf
and a little Hitler
by the time we met him.
I was put on tipping –
emptying the sacks of mail
onto the conveyor
and then elbowing the sack
to make sure nothing was left in.
I later learned that tipping
is the most knackering job.
I worked over five hours
without a break
and whenever I stopped
Sol was right there
raising his eyebrows.
Once he marched over
and tipped two sacks
at the same time
but I had seen this kind
of management before.

These Work Boots

He looked down at my trainers.
"They said I had to wear boots,"
he said, "Paid out for these
and my feet are killing me."
He moaned about these work boots
for the whole shift, hour after hour,
on and on about these boots.
Finally, he said, "Next fucking time
I'm coming in wearing my shorts
and I'm going to wear flip-flops
and if any fucker says out to me
I'm just going to twat them."
Little victories, he knew about that.
That's what got you through.
That and having a good moan
at anyone prepared to listen.

The Last Post

About nine bells all the men
started wheeling the post out on stage
as fast as they could manage.
For once I felt like working hard
so I pushed more, walked quicker
saw the pleasure in the manager's eyes
as I kept on pushing, pulling
sweating and grafting
knowing that come 10.15pm
I would be walking out
onto the cool of Oldham Road
and never, ever coming back.

Mancunian Spring

Below the yellow trams,
the wind rips through
fat busted fingers,
around fingerprint cups
and springs, as the towers rise
above the birds of Pomona.
Glass shines with rain
and sends a whistle
through the brick piles,
along the haunted canal,
across the legs of joggers,
through the lumps of scrap,
above the shattered pavements,
through the concrete and steel,
in and around the oiled shack
of the men in *Mancunian Spring*.

Commuter Sunlight

The birds in commuter sunlight lift off glass
as the turbines whirl white on the hill.

On this tram all eyes and ears are stimulated
by scenes not visible in the window.

The good thing about getting up this early
is seeing the sunrise making a view into a picture

and turning the capitalist impulse into birds' wings
that rise above the re-branded tram stops.

Most beautiful of all is the red brick
of the old cotton mills still standing

how that red is given a glow by the sun
how the toil is a deafened memory.

Some languid souls are lounging in sight
within flats now spinning with sunlight.

The Peregrine

Standing in Cathedral Gardens, in a whirlpool of wind, we positioned the tripod and the telescope. Though May, the wind was cold and the fluffy peregrine kept blowing off the table. The box of pin badges remained, and I fished out a kestrel.

The other volunteer talked all day, fuelled by Red Bull and cigarettes. She had her nose pierced, seemed a bit mad, and I fancied her. But I had to stop trying it on with women in their twenties.

I focused the telescope on each of the red ARNDALE letters, hoping to see the fastest animal on earth, but each time I looked there was just the reminder of commerce.

There were no sightings either on the cathedral or the Premier Inn, and the great summit of the CIS tower glinted with sunlight, but was absent of falcons.

All day long, people of differing nationalities passed on the way to the football museum. A great number of homeless travelled by, lugging rucksacks and trailing unfurled sleeping bags all frayed at the edges.

More than a few people stopped to talk at our table, and all of them were lonely, not quite knowing the extent.

I sat in the car, drank from a flask and ate my lemon curd sandwiches. Looking at the roof of Chetham's, all I saw were pigeons.

It was late afternoon, the sun floating from orange to pink. The crowds had died down, the football museum was closed, and with one last look up, I saw J.A. Baker's bird, like a flash of meaning from a dream.

The Etihad

Strange how it is, the lack of atmosphere
not a rose-tinted patch on the Kippax.
You go in and take your seat and you feel
like your childhood is missing.
                              Where once
you had climbed the stairs and walked through
a picture frame of green to feel vibration,
buzz, singing, seething sound, under a vast
corrugated roof where the rain never touched
you, now you sat in your padded seat
the bloke from somewhere south of Watford
moaning about Toure for the whole game –
Toure the best midfielder since Bell –
and the rain blew in under the stand
and over you, and the away fans made most
noise every game, but even their songs
were like a memory of the atmosphere
when you were standing, when you loved
a victory, when it was cheaper to get in
and there was a blue turnstile and a cage
but most of all when there was tension
and there was edge.
                    And although it still
means equally as much to many of you now
you don't express it, and there isn't the chanting
that coursed through you when you joined in
and that took you out of yourself, made you forget
your week, the same as every other week
and helped get life out of your system
showed you still had life in your system.

Women Grow Old in Factories

With her t-shirt and smile
she was nothing to them

but an immigrant.
Her youth and hard work

meant nothing to them.
She was one of many voices

on their phones asking for work
week in, week out

doing day shifts, night shifts
evening shifts. No sick pay.

Nothing but the eyes of managers
already fucking their wives.

The same kinds calling out
against all the immigrants.

As kids wash up on beaches
and women grow old in factories.

Sonny Rollins on the Williamsburg Bridge

High above the trains, with his golden gleaming sax, the jazzman flies beyond all the hotshot commuters, and the two-time losers, the bruisers. He plays beyond his brain, the notes sailing out across the river, the bright blazing river. New York City let him be. Let him play to the sky, the boats and the trains. Keep your commerce and your wars. Your wars will go on. You will never listen, but someone might, some little kid not yet conned by guns and money.

To Let

Comes the night, turning the red patterned clouds blurred by the broken glazing into a cold blue of skies, the same outline of building against the immensity, and the tall trees through which the sun falls in a golden pattern caused by the twinkling of the leaves. And now, in silent suburban night, I hear the cough of the man next door, the beer bottles in the bag of the boy across the hall, and the sweet smell of weed from the Irish guy downstairs with his walls of DVD's.

This whole building is absent of women and there's just the mother over the road, with her children and her Beagle and the Egyptian statues. The street darkens, and the TO LET signs for the lonely people turn orange in the light of the streetlamps, and the streets wait for car thieves and foxes, and the only sounds are the deep muted sounds of the bathroom fans as the solitary men get up to piss in the night.

Ragged Curtains

Through the ragged net curtain
shines the green glow of the tennis court.

Closer, there's the flickering candle
of a neighbour who pads around

barefoot on these summer nights,
sometimes bending near the candle

and showing her cleavage to me
through her own ragged curtain.

In this building
the doors open and close all the time

and there are whirling fans in the bathrooms.
But sometimes, with the TV off,

I stare through the ragged net curtain
that covers the broken double glazing

in the front window, and see a red sky
behind the silhouette of a magpie.

The Kestrel

Getting up the hill was exhausting
but once there we caught breath.

We had to cross a road, strangely,
before entering a field of horses.

I was calm then and they came to me.
We stroked them on that hillside of mud.

Passing beyond that field I looked up,
spotted the kestrel, hovering there.

Passing you the glasses you watched
and it was a joy to pass that on to you.

We continued up the hill, reached the top,
walked through the wind at the edge.

You enjoyed that wind blowing over you
as we looked across to hills and water.

Continuing our walk, we passed by the hotel
where my friend had had his honeymoon.

We turned a corner and the sky was filled
with a black spring of jackdaws.

Behind us, on the other side of the hill,
the kestrel swooped down for prey.

At Laddow Rocks

Low sun's heat through skeleton trees.
A grey squirrel sprinting over limbs.
Woodpeckers in a thrashing chase.

A house covered in holly and smoke.
The path from Oldham filled with crows.

A brief flash of deer eyes in forest.
Stoodley Pike beyond the trees and hills
like a thumbs up from a distant child.

Later, ducks climbing the hillside
and then the reservoir wall
from which they splashed into the glinting.

My own feet in cold-clutching water,
I watched again the languid loops
of the distant raven's wings.

Lastly, by the rocks of Laddow Rocks,
I looked at the water's curling descent
towards Crowden, and scanned the sky
for more ravens on the valley's other side.

A faint whistle made me look
towards the cut of sky above
where a buzzard made its exit,
turning red wings from the sunset.

The Sheep of the South Tyne Valley

I remember the sheep
of the South Tyne Valley.
Not in that way, you pervert.

I remember how they buried
their heads in deep snow
to get at the grass beneath.

How they lined up behind
drystone walls that blocked the wind.

How the farmer at Plenmeller
got a quid per live lamb
he delivered.

I remember those lambs bouncing
in fields below Willimoteswick Castle.

I remember being relaxed
by their calming presence

in contrast to the skittish antics
of crazy eyed cows
with their stomping and slipping hooves.

I remember how the mothers
stood protecting their lambs

and I remember realizing
I would never have children.

Curlew Calls

When I walked the moors
of the South Tyne Valley
not knowing anyone
within 150 miles
I hugged the very call
of the curlew.

I watched them lift together
from fields by the banks
of the river.
Once I peered over a drystone wall
and saw one right there
before me.

Flying on my bike
over bumping tarmac
down the hill into Beltingham
they were burbling there, in the air.
The first time I heard them
was on Coombs moss
in Derbyshire.
I wasn't so alone then
and hindsight makes those calls
sound like a portent.

Kissing Gate

Kissing gate, I found you alone and walked towards the skies by myself. Waterfalls fell below kestrels. Ferries were tiny islands in the sound. There were meadow pipits and falcons in the summit clouds. Tossed oatcakes brought ravens. They tumbled superfluously. On the silent heights everything slipped into the chasms and my strides were mountain flowers filled with greasy, happy frogs.

The water through the glen was a silver tie on a hotel floor some two hundred miles south, on a morning after a night before when they ran out of Guinness. And on that morning we woke together naked, the sweat dried on us and I wandered swinging to the windows, opened the curtains and marvelled at you in the sunlight.

Moths

Today, though we've never met, I imagined you swinging towards me, that dress of flowers peeled off to reveal all your wobbling wonder.

Sometime in the last century I heard you read your poetry, and you wore a corset spun with gold, and your words lifted in exquisite patterns like rarefied moths to the light.

The Pusher

It has been pushing people in,
under the bridges as they stagger down

the towpath in a chamber of graffiti;
under the great towers of the gasworks,

near where the pipeline crosses the water;
at the locks, where takeaway boxes float

by Canal Street and the bodies splash
into neon. It has been by rivers too,

at the weir under the road by the meadow.
Don't walk down by the water at night.

You might end up tangled in the undertow,
dragged down by the nine to five.

Eagles in the Red Sky

I was standing in the water
cleaning my cooking pan
with a clump of wet heather.

My mate said, 'You're in
your element here, aren't you?'
He was right, I was.

I could have been in a kilt
with woolly socks up to my knees
and a tweed jacket shining in the sun.

The mountains were reflected
in the still, silent waters of the loch
and there were eagles in the red sky.

Turning Up the Volume

When he was drunk he had no idea about volume. So he sat there and turned her up and she roared like flames or coastline. He sipped his clinking drink and felt its throttling burn before the scenes slipped into green and the horses leaped the fences, their chestnut forms rippling through the rural vista. He flashed back to their first time in the sack when her pale body enveloped him and the dark room filled with starlight, the time they stormed a drunken fairground groping at candy floss and hip flasks of gin and whisky, and the gold coast morning in the last century when they pulled back flowered curtains and saw heatwaves. He watched the ceremony from the shade of condemned trees. Saw the following years of selfless, clinging hugging, the slacking of her jowls and the progress of her starred children. He saw the shining rewards of television, the vacant semblance of success, her choices exemplified by the greying and drying out of her once lustrous hair. He turned up the volume beyond where it could go and saw her in a purple pistachio of memory, her eyes green as the star fished depths of coral, her smile an emblazoned slice, a knifed rose, her lips a giving, softened sunset moistened by liquor and kisses. With the memory of her music painting the walls like the sun paints the old buildings of broken towns, he lifted his sodden face back and listened as the glorious fragments of his bolted life consoled him with arias and tone poems.

The Grand Old Gardens of a Country House in Summer Bloom

He was the bashful man sticking sweating fingers in for recognition and having to ask reception to let him through the glass doors. His muted 'thank you' could have dropped birds from trees. On that first day she had watched from the window of their adjoining rooms as he was pinned down by six students and had his mobile phone taken out of his pocket. She watched again as the principal arrived, a man as tall as a sunflower in August and with the same range of practical uses. They pinned him down too, and amid a whirl of cackling, a multi-coloured art work spiralled into flame, the alarms kicked in, and the rest of the afternoon was spent at the assembly point making something of the March sun, hugging it like a breast. She was like the grand old gardens of a country house in summer bloom and she always waited for the supply teachers. This newly broken man was the seventh in recent weeks. Once she got her early retirement she'd be gone too. They stood in the staff room together and she pulled him into a hug. They could all take this pain and save it as a memory for waking on crystal mornings on the west coast, the sound of the shingle coddling their broken hearts in sheaves of silver leaf.

Golden Animals

His watch had the large face of a child and glimmered in the heat haze. Glancing at it over and over as though it were a child in his care he traced his old footsteps down the rice littered boulevard. He noted the makes and models of the dilapidated cars and the spaces where other cars could be. Finally turning the corner, he saw her there behind the bars in a dress hewn from stars and shoes the colour of trees. He set his shimmering watch and she opened the gilded padlocks. They embraced and might have stood there clasped in perpetuity. All around them inside the cage there were little golden animals biting at their legs and mewling for attention. On a vast cinema-like screen the golden animals watched adults acting like stoned children. With the golden animals occupied, our two sweating dupes shadow played among the striped shade of the bars, rehearsing the shapes of super 8 performances from a time when the future was a painted ocean. With the very bars ticking to the echo of his vast, childlike watch, they commingled and sought out each other's bliss. Prostrate under their cover of stripes, they listened to each other's breathing, felt the rocking of respective chests, and heard with accomplished dread the sea breeze and sound of waves that secreted in at the time of their half-parting. The golden animals turned, wild eyed and pleading, before springing on them with bared teeth like the maniacal bears of CGI.

Ravens on Cir Mohr

Pieces of broken bread
bring ravens closer,
floating over Cir Mohr
down to The Saddle
in flaps of heavy wing.
Dropping wholemeal
by my feet I walk
until ravens come over
the corrie for more,
dark purple beaks
before them in flight,
black wings brushing
against blue skies
as they play among
the thermals.

Oystercatchers at Seabank

As the tide comes in
the big seal and little seal allow
water to lift them off rocks.
When the water stills,
swans come slowly,
floating in line
waiting for brushstrokes.
An old poet paces across gravel
in her garden. The streetlight
emerges. The blue light
of the lighthouse flashes,
signalling oystercatchers
in orange mayhem.

Jellyfish at Sandbraes

They sit flat on the sand
waiting for runners' fast feet
but nobody comes before tide

*

In the sea at Sandbraes
jellyfish flat until the tide
leap up to float under blue

*

Hanging like a lampshade
the jellyfish at Sandbraes
float in wait for swimmers

Light on Lamlash

The last night of the week
I sink into bed before eleven.
In the rented room, thick curtains
barely cover sash windows
and the fading light of Lamlash.
Echoes of the shore filter through:
brushing of water on rock,
swan's progress, heron flight,
curlew's stirring beak,
the contemplation of Buddhists
across the water.

Kestrels at Kilpatrick Point

Oystercatchers cause a fuss
until I pass into foxgloves
by the coastal path.

King's Cave is swept by sparkles
and shaded in blue as I stumble
over a hard hat from Felixstowe.

Two kestrels spiral
around Kilpatrick Point,
above cliffs and preacher's caves.

The Tide

The tide goes out slowly
over a shoreline of rock pools
where curlews dip for food
and seaweed is draped over stone
like a memory.
In wave after wave
the water leaves the shore,
uncovering rocks that are still there,
and the bay empties,
becomes dark and dazzling
in evening sunlight.

Cormorants at Blackwaterfoot

Who tailored such suits,
hanging from the shoulders
of these inky, oily birds
like the shining garb
of their own solicitors?

Was it Arran fisherman,
denied the liberty of waves
by a black plague of sea crows?

A Vision of Herons

It seemed that even the sky
of Lochranza was green
in the dripping evening.
Walking along the coast road
in the silence – save only for
the occasional peeping oystercatcher
or scavenging hoodie crow –
I looked at all the jackdaws
on the shoreline, and a stately swan,
bright white against the green of
bushes and bracken. Finally
I was off the 9-5 treadmill.
As if to confirm it,
two grey herons came heavy-
winged into the green sky.

The Fishing Zone

The curve of the bay
is my eyesight returning
among church bells.

The silver shifting platter
of the sea serves up
birds in images of freedom.

The slick ripple of the
introverted tide comes in
like age and goes out again.

Today I feel like the
heron, hassled by gulls
in the fishing zone.

Seals at Kildonan

[for J. Barret Wolf]

As we'd seen enough
he could make his joke
about counting them off
and ending on 'The
Seventh Seal'. They stayed
there, not for us, but because
they were warm in the sunshine.
And the grunts of the big one
seemed to confirm it, as he
rolled around on the rock
surrounded by the grey glimmer
of the other seals and the sea.

Rock House Fell

The burn runs
under a little bridge
on Rock House Fell
and I look down
at the water
to see a weasel
reaching from sparkles
into a trap, its rotten image
fixed under a sky
of horse flies.

Goldfinch in Tow House

A little dot sits on the wire
among the smoke of fog.
The North Pennines are gone,
the Newcastle train goes by.

Yellow and red and black
and white emerges, the little head
of the goldfinch twitching
as burns run quickly to the river.

Prudhoe Fisherman

The train from Carlisle
approaches Prudhoe, passes close
to a wide stretch of the Tyne.

As the train lines curve
the view from the window
affords a straight-on sight of the water.

In the distance there's a stationary torso,
a shadowed stop in morning movement.
A woman from Oxford

charms with anecdotes culminating
in an account of her first husband;
a fisherman. Canada geese pass by

as she tells her daughter of blouses
that will last her until she dies.

The Black Mount

[for Phil]

We passed the Clashgour Hut
and ascended with light packs
to camp near the summit of Stob Ghabar.

We put up the tent and weightless
walked on to Stob Choire Odhair
to look out across the pools of Rannoch Moor.

Coming back to Stob Ghabar
we sat on Karrimats in the sun
watching seven ravens spiralling.

It rained all night and in the morning
we took the tent down from inside,
and walked slip-sliding off the summit,

dodging frogs on our descent
through smudged paint of wildflowers
to Rannoch Moor, where we crossed the River Ba.

At the Inveroran Hotel
we sat in the bar at the back
scratching and smiling and drinking,

until a town planner from Walsall
unclipped his bike clips and bored us
through round after round.

Horse

[after James Wright]

There is a horse behind the sightscreen,
silent in the cold sunlight.
The wind is moving clouds quickly
over South Head, where icing lines
of snow linger beside black rocks and
buffets of green.
The horse is brown
with a white blaze between her eyes.
She seems to move with resignation
and regret.
Then she begins to race
around the paddock mocking me.
I think that if I sit beside this window
for long enough, the hills themselves
might just break into laughter.

Bugsworth Full Moon

Casually pulling
the curtains
across the beginnings
of dusk, its silver
bright shine
hits my brain,
sends the curtains
back open in a flash
and causes a 'wow'
in response
to the dazzle.
It is hard to imagine
that men
landed on it
when its magic circle
seems something
too dreamlike for surfaces.
I put on my fleece
and hiking boots,
turn off the news,
step out
into the silvered dusk,
walk Western Lane,
climb the hill
up to Portobello Farm
stand closer
and more bedazzled
by the stark clarity
of silver above,
wonder at its effect
on the animals.

Cows on Barren Clough

Below the jackdaw trees
white cows rummage and roam.

One curves for low branches,
another comes down the hill in a Z.

Others eat grass together,
heads down, slow as clouds.

Lagg to Tarbet

[for Uncle Rod]

At Lagg, the German from the campsite catches us up on his yellow bike. We discuss the impossibility of reaching Barnhill, where Orwell wrote *1984*. Stefan gives out digestive biscuits. Uncle Rod soon speeds off up the steep climb. I follow him and Stefan up the hill. I wear heavy walking boots and the frame on the hire bike is too small. I struggle up the hill to where tall trees shade the road. Freewheeling around a series of hairpin bends we drop into Tarbet, where the island is at its narrowest point. Crofters came that way from Colonsay.

yellow bike
and blue bikes
– freewheeling

Haiku Sequence

By the tram stop
On St Werburgh's Road
Unpicked blackberries

Young boy kicking a ball
Outside the football museum
– will he play for City?

Outside the museum
A man in his fifties
Falls off a skateboard

The wino with
The broken-hearted face
On the curry mile

White roses –
And magpies picking
For worms

Two Pictures

Four Boats

We can see three boats on the shore. Another boat, a smaller one, can't yet be seen. All are tied together with ropes. In the background, a bird leaves its flying shadow on the water as a moment passing. The rest of the boats are all floating and apparently secure, while the other four wait for the water. The masts of the floating boats rise into the air together like spikes, spikes to burst the dark clouds in the sky. To the right of the picture the horizon is light and when the tide comes the weather comes and the four boats will float together then, whatever that weather.

Two Boats

A rusted old boat sits leaning to one side on the concrete shore, the flat sea stretching out before it. A little boat sits on the concrete behind the rusted old boat. We can't tell if they are two of the four boats from before, or if only one of them is the same. The sky is largely bright but we don't know if that is weather coming or gone. There are things in the water but we can't make them out. We don't know if the tide is coming or going because at the moment we can't see any tide at all. We don't know if the water will come in and set them free from the concrete to bob and float on the sea below the sky or if they will sit together on the concrete always.

The Whole Enchilada (Santa Cruz to Salinas)

Moss Landing
oranges and apples
green and yellow fields
Pacific Ocean
a field of shimmering sprinklers
sand dunes and breaking waves
Reservation Road
white houses
a dusty baseball diamond
deep green trees
auburn scrub
white sea birds
boarded-up and splintered dust houses
mile high Christmas trees
blue and grey skies
a message written in twigs
Del Ray and Laguna
stars and stripes breaking the shore
fairgrounds and playgrounds
Pacific Grove and Carmel
a house made of roses
white walls and brown roofs
turquoise doorways
balconies full if children
easy street paisanos
Monterey romances
do-re-mi men
grog shops
Wells Fargo in pink
boats moored on a roundabout

red leaves on brown
whale fest
liquors and soda
beach volleyball
lakes of geese
parrots on a rooftop
a mongoose in the sand
a driveway of grass
vineyards
pink and orange houses
eagles and horses
Quail Ridge
white picket fences
tierras and sierras
fog in the valley
Toro Park
acacia trees
cooling towers
pathways up hills
Spreckels Blvd
pyramid houses
foil field markers
fields of soil, fields of dust
tractors and trailers
pipes and petrol pumps
a million-mile wide valley
hills swathed in mist
San Joaquin Street
smog stations
Salinas, Salinas, Salinas ...

Pomona Kestrel

Pomona kestrel, you hover above
the great foundations of glass towers
you swoop and turn and revolve
your reds and browns, but soon
you will be lost behind photographs
that won a competition in the Apple Store.

When the piebald paperwork says,
'On a scale of one to three'
will we all whiz through, ticking '2'?

The Old Goat

It had been six years since I'd walked that moor,
followed it around to Ladder Hill and descended
along the footpath. The right of way that took me
through an enclosure for goats, before a field,
then a tiny tunnel beneath the train line to Buxton.

Those years before I'd taken a photo of a horny goat
and the little bastard had butted me in the shins.
Here he was again, greyer of beard, yellower of eye.
As I reached for my phone to take another photo
he came at me again, chin tucked in, horns out-thrust.

That day, same as the other day, I'd walked five hours
without a map under skies where birds were sailing.

The Blue Bell, Warrington

This quiet observation of strangers
as clouds cross the tables.

Golden ale, a golden light,
like sunshine across the optics.

A golden woman too,
walking through the shadows of attraction,
unsated by the lamb shank and bitter.

Monday afternoon in a town I don't know.
The time and place for the poverty poet.

One more pint and these clouds
will coalesce into paintings.

Burning

I was up on the hill one time, covered in smoke, the burning ground blasting me as my neighbour stood there like an astronaut and you watched us both from heaven. In the sun and the heat-licking wind my boozy head helped in the forgetting of everything and I walked across the smoking ground towards a new vista, where by sunset the smoke had gone, replaced by the honking of a hundred geese. I followed their shadows towards a house where I had been the year before, and there were holes in the roof, open doorways and empty grates.

Creative Writing

Trapped in their endless days, the creative writing teachers bemoan their lack of time while I nibble crackers and scribble with a pen stained by crocodile tears. If only I could find another job where I work out how not to work. I've had many.

There's room enough for books in here and enough technology for voices. If I can keep it switched off for long enough I can go back to my silver volumes of Steinbeck, say hello to the old boy like he's my third grandad, and kip to the snooker in the afternoons.

I had it sussed in the council flat, reading Bukowski in the sunset and draining Budweiser as my thirties slipped away. In my forties now, what's changed? Love came and went like the books told me it would, and I swopped Budweiser for Whyte and Mackay. Yesterday a mate of mine said, "Creative Writing? What's that, like calligraphy?"

Cortez Postcard

On the boat again with Ed, we chase the tidal race and drink and notate, and trace the Spanish sunsets with burned fingers and whisky lips. In the low lapping currents, so different to Monterey, we drift and bob and sing until the moon plays across the headland and we retreat to the cabin and scribble in our salty notebooks about the universe and beer. Ed cracks open the six-pack and we lie back on our beds and talk, the shadow of the swinging lantern on us, and all the glistening fish a knock on wood away.

The Compass

How can I, who drew tits and cocks in condensation, ripped curtains and threw paper balls at teachers and into their cups of tea, even contemplate cover supervisor work? I who once sat and watched a supply teacher get stabbed in the arse by an errant compass as Damian Harris toyed with a loose thread on the poor sod's pants. I who when asked to go and fetch a dictionary from another classroom came back with twenty and deliberately tripped, throwing them across the room so that they slid towards the feet of the hopeless man in the cheap suit who didn't know anybody's name.

Hair & Beauty, Withington

I can see the blonde girl in the unisex salon, standing behind the counter, fiddling with her bra strap and gold necklace, looking at sunlight on cars as they pass through Withington. She bends and shows her brown cleavage, then looks at her watch: it is 4:59. She bends over again to pack up her stuff and then goes next door to the *Canadian Charcoal Pit* where the man behind the counter stares at her breasts.

'I'm Done'

She tells me that she drives;
goes to Asda in the car
and just sits there.
"It's the only way," she says.

She shows me her phone.
There are diary entries.
I look through them and
one says simply, "I'm done."

I saw her once, many years ago.
I was waiting for the 219
as she walked through
Ashton bus station.

Nothing had happened to her
and she was magnificent.

The Lift

So, she's been round. Pinched my nipples quite painfully as I kissed hers. She shoved her breasts in my face; suffocated me with their might. Not all of my days hold such pleasure, but we both deserved a bit of fun. She asked me about possessive apostrophes, leafed through my books, found a fictional character with her name. Her legs shone like marble. Her high heels clattered on the stairs when she left. The heels were a soft red, the same as her nails. There wasn't a trace of hair, not so much as a vague roughness of stubble on her legs. She was sober today and didn't cry. She is lifting herself out of something, I know it.

Birdsongs

The sunset has
painted a Rothko

on my wall.
I turn to see

the setting sun.
It is coming across

the sea like
a trail of birds.

Blackbird evening;
blackbird, sunlit-

singing evening.
Can I not

just sit and listen,
sit and watch?

This orange evening
of birdsongs

is so marvellously
absent of politics.

Ice Cream

She's away for the night
and so he gets stuck into
the salted caramel ice cream
they got from the Maker's Market
that he hated the idea of
going to.

He no longer drinks, in fact
he walked past three pubs
and two supermarkets on the
way home from work.

He almost went into the Co-Op
for more ice cream; the Swedish
stuff they got that time,
which had no price on,
and that she said they could get
if it was less than three quid.

In the Gemini Café

I'm in the Gemini Café
on my break from work
and I see this lad come in
and he has reddish hair
and a patchy beard
and a cheap suit, and he's
taken off his jacket and while
I sit facing the window
he sits with his back to it
and he's reading his book
and drinking his coffee
and then he starts looking
at himself in the mirror
and I think that
we are kind of the same,
trying to get something
out of the work day
and though I'm more relaxed
than he is, he's younger,
I've been longer in jobs
where the air you breathe
comes at break time.